180 Keys

To Greatness

By: Shanelle Woodard

Copyright 2017

Woodard Holdings Publishing, LLC

ISBN-10:0-692-92696-8

ISBN-13:978-0-692-92696-3

Dedication

Jeffery, Key, Mary, Sky'lee, Paola

Thanks for keeping me focused!

Contents

Introduction

Chapter 1: It was said

Chapter 2: Then it passed

Chapter 3: Then time moved

Chapter 4: Then it was life

Chapter 5: Then there was 180 Keys

Chapter 6: And then?

Introduction

Introduction

This book is a guide through a journey of life that is called wisdom. If you understand and properly use the keys you will be wise and guided through this journey called life. Walk with the purest intentions.

Chapter 1:

It was said

Chapter 1:

It was said

Key #1

I think the strongest people in the world are children.

Key #2

You are born whole, the world through time takes you apart piece by piece until you feel you need validation for being born. But your birth was your validation. You were made whole before you came out of the womb. So why do you need manmade things to tell you, you ARE?

Key #3

Fight by direction, not by emotion.

Key #4

Everybody sees differently, but blindly.

Key #5

Everybody's vessel is built for different journey's.

Key #6

Never waste your time with someone who doesn't even like being around themselves.

Key #7

Consistency is the father of opportunities.

Key #8

React how you want genius is genius let it live.

Key #9

Be influenced by great philosophy not a lyric.

Key #10

Corrupt individuals make your world toxic, keep them out.

Key #11

If the sun shines upon you don't drench yourself in shade continue to shine.

Key #12

Negativity and fear is the worse disease to a child.

Key #13

A sad man makes nobody happy he is only good at isolating himself from happiness.

Key#14

Stop being scared to try and fail because of other people's opinions of what you did.

Key #15

Be able to see the big pictures in order to make the best decisions.

Key#16

Use your mind to observe so that you can direct yourself accordingly for that current situation.

Key#17

Control your awareness, direct your mind.

Key#18

Will power can be develop to better your fight against choosing your wants over your needs.

Key#19

Watch who you invest your energy into.

Key#20

Energy is a firm resource, ask the question of why I should put my energy into this person, place, or thing?

Chapter 2:

Then it passed

Chapter 2:

Then it passed

Key#21

Be clear on what's important and all your focus will finally be concentrated.

Key#22

There's two sides judging and evaluating. Prefer to evaluate then judge.

Key#23

It's not just the individual, it's the opportunity you leave the individual to rob you. If you lock the door they can't get in.

Key #24

Don't call yourself a leader if you never successfully ran a household.

Key #25

If you are spending $1000 or more for a holiday called Christmas for unnecessary material items that don't empower the recipient than you don't understand the meaning of Christmas.

Key #26

Peace begins with you not the man walking beside you.

Key #27

If you don't survey your surroundings you will be stuck in a situation you may not be able to get out of.

Key #28

Stop judging somebody for their physical appearance, for even physical appearance is the teacher of ignorance.

Key #29

Don't work the man who already works hard, harder, fire the man that doesn't work hard and hire one that works just as hard, or else you will have a disgruntled work environment.

Key #30

Build a team for the life of the business, not for the life of a short plan.

Key #31

It's not about the details in the plan it's about the people who execute the plan.

Key #32

The concern shouldn't be the fiat currency but the currency of the future. Everything must go extinct.

Key #33

Hold your head high even in failure, because you know you were the only one in the room to have the audacity to try.

Key #34

Sometimes you have to put the gun and knife in their hands and ask them to do what they gotta do in life in order to see where you really stand with the person.

Key #35

Don't be bound by vanity.

Key #36

With tragedy comes a teaching moment.

Key #37

You are the easiest person you fool.

Key #38

Gray hair is a crown but what kind of crown is it? One of burden, or wisdom, of destruction of one's self or so on?

Key #39

When someone ask you what is your time worth, you should answer with this; your life.

Key #40

Money or the lack of makes people reveal their true self.

Chapter 3:

Then time moved

Chapter 3:

Then time moved

Key #41

The tragedy in the truth is the reality of life.

Key #42

Stop with the if it ain't me it can't be them.

Everybody deserve the good life not just you.

key #43

Stop worrying about the obvious and start worrying about the not so obvious.

key #44

Know when it's over before the silence hits the room.

key #45

Stop expecting things from people who don't expect to live to see tomorrow.

key #46

Don't look for the person beside you to be your rock, learn how to stand monumentally on your own and expand your strength upon the next.

key #47

It's your responsibility you birthed it but you want the weight of the walk on someone else's shoulders, well i'm sorry the journey is to make your shoulders stronger, not to slump someone else's over.

key #48

It's not about how much you go through but how much you smile through it that makes you different.

key #49

Life is a simple plan of time that can be ran through or enjoyed through, make it a joyful journey.

key #50

Every person you speak truth to in life should be present to celebrate your life in death, or else you missed the point of life.

key #51

We are not here to collect material things, we are here to induce change and love.

key #52

Stop thinking about getting support, and think about supporting the upbringing of a child less fortunate than you were.

key #53

You think its cute blowing your whole paycheck till you see real struggle, and the people you was trying to impress say they can't help you then what?

key #54

Handouts lead to more handouts and it becomes a horrible

habit.

key #55

Destiny, don't fight her off embrace. She is only the answer to all the good and bad you have done thus far.

key #56

Don't let the love of yourself, blind you from yourself.

key #57

Don't just pray for someone be the support that keeps them fighting.

key #58

Build a lineage bank, not a corporation bank that cares nothing about your lineage.

key #59

Stop seeing with your eyes and pay attention with your god given senses. Use them as you were born to.

key #60

Empower your circle and you will never go broke.

Chapter 4:

Then it was life

Chapter 4:

Then it was life

key #61

The history is already written just follow it.

Key #62

Play the quiet fool in the room, till the real fool reveals himself.

key #63

There is no tomorrow, it is not guaranteed so live your dreams today not tomorrow.

Key #64

Activism is not to be t.v. famous but to evoke change in the hearts of our fellow brethren.

key #65

sacrifice trumps selfishness everyday.

key #66

The wool over your eyes was knitted by you, now will you be the one to rip it away and see clearly?

key #67

The picture is beautiful but what about the frame it comes in?

key #68

Know what you have to do to get into the proper position.

key #69

Watch who you call your second in command they may be trying to take your position.

Key #70

Stop spending all your money for a holiday that will not pay for your kids college education. just a little is good enough.

Key #71

Tradition shouldn't be the definition of when you come around family, or show love to family. The holiday is only another day.

Key #72

Your thoughts and habits determine if you will have a future.

Key #73

You knew the situation was going to be hot but you was so thirsty you got burnt. Grow patience and wait for it to cool over.

Key #74

The best feeling in the world is to own your own destiny.

Key #75

Power don't make respect, respect maker's power.

Key #76

Don't be scared to self-educate yourself.

Key #77

Work to serve others and put yourself into a position to employ others.

Key #78

Don't fall out over your significant other, they are the other for a reason let them go. They are only human, your love for yourself should be stronger.

Key #79

The poverty is programmed in your mind not your pockets. The wealth of information you build up grows your opportunities to make income.

key #80

If you sell death, your life will be even shorter than planned.

Chapter 5:

Then there was 180 Keys

Chapter 5:

Then there was 180 Keys

Key #81

You can't be in five places at one time but give the perception that you can, and people will think before they act when it concerns you.

Key #82

When the man ask for help, extend your hand and guide him. If he doesn't ask for your help why do you keep extending your hands, and becoming frustrated when the person still keeps messing up?

Key #83

Be passionate about the truth because there is nothing beyond it.

Key #84

Some thing's should be left inside time.

Key #85

Stop reaching out for people who don't want to be touched. Save your genius for somebody who will accept it.

Key #86

Don't ask to be accepted by others, you are the only person you need to acknowledge.

Key #87

Autobiography your own story, don't let somebody do it for you.

Key #88

Your mother is the most loyalists person you will ever meet in your life. Women have the natural emotion of loyalty.

Key #89

The word broke is a word, your actions make it a reality.

Key #90

Intelligence will never trump common sense on any given day.

Key #91

Don't try to lead a show with terrible supporting actors because you still won't win a emmy with your performance, because everybody else's performance around you was lackluster.

Stop trying to lead a group of people who don't want to work for the betterment of the group. Put a new supporting cast around you who do want to put in the work.

Key #92

We go through new years but we still love the same god. It's still the same time we just had to define it for hope. But god is hope so why we steady trying to define time?

Key #93

The legacy is built during your journey in life, in the after life you should be given your physical crown and wings for what joy you put on earth.

Key #94

You have the answer to your question in your hands but you too lazy to open your hands to write the answer.

Stop being your own roadblock in your success.

Key #95

Don't live in the depression and look for someone to bring you out of it, motivate yourself and bring the light into your life yourself.

Key #96

They love to see you fail but hate to see you succeed misery in the name of company is not the life but the death of you.

Key #97

Currency doesn't make you happy happiness makes you currency. Happiness gives you everything you need.

Key #98

Be still and let the rest of the world run in panic, you be your island of peace when the world around falls apart.

Key #99

Never laugh in an ambitious person's face, you never know what fire you may ignite.

Key #100

The brain is sustainable and information to feed it is easily obtainable, so why do we not feed the mind hourly?

Chapter 6:

And then?

Chapter 6:

And then?

Key #101

The more we stick together the more we win.

Key #102

Out think them, not out work them. Don't over extend your energy when your biggest muscle is your mind.

Key #103

In certain situations always have a witness around.

Key #104

Don't buy into something that won't buy into you.

Key #105

Yes, when it rains it pours and you can't control the rain sometimes however you build the umbrella as big as you want to protect you from the rain.

Key #106

The truth is the reality of life.

Key #107

They laugh at what they don't understand, allow them the room to do so and allow that laughter to be your fuel of ambition.

Key #108

Let your purpose be your means of survival.

Key #109

Love the man who doesn't love himself, and maybe one day he will learn love comes from thy-self.

Key #110

Only through faith and love can one man become greatness.

Key #111

You should find peace inside your home. Not outside of it.

Key #112

Never allow your genius to be restricted. Use your full potential no matter the cost.

Key #113

Put the spirit of love that god gave you in everything that you do. Even if you have a distaste for what you do.

Key #114

Don't walk through that door for yourself, walk through that door to change someone's life. Be the giver of gifts not the receiver of them.

Key #115

If it is his time, don't interject in god's summons.

Key #116

Your home is your sanctuary treat it as if to walk through the doors of a place of worship. You should feel spiritually awakened and at peace with life.

Key #117

Don't hold back who you are, because of who they are. We live so that we can be.

Key #118

Don't recur debts, and don't in-debt.

Key #119

The future is five minutes from now not five to ten years later.

Key #120

When you're thinking you're making movements and you're still standing in the same place. Figure out why your legs aren't moving.

Key #121

Life and death, there is no death once a legacy of service is set forth throughout your time in the vessel of the body. You never die once your body stops moving.

Key #122

A man's silent thoughts is the true depth of his soul.

Key #123

Stop working to tell somebody you work, work for results of change to someone less fortunates life.

Key #124

Once you get the taste of good water in your mouth, don't allow anyone to take it away. Stop trying to continue to drink out of the poisoned fountain, you are worth all things great no matter who you are.

Key #125

Every day is a blank canvas, and you are the only one who can turn that blank canvas into a masterpiece of life, love, and peace.

Key #126

Stop allowing people to build a box around you, you will never be put in a box if you stay out of their box.

Key #127

Turning your back on one of god's children is like turning your back on god himself.

Key #128

What does it matter you did it, you ego driven person, what matters is you accomplishing the purpose god birth you with.

Key #129

We were born with two hands, one hand of god and one hand of human error. Use the hand of god more than the hand of error.

Key #130

Just want to help, not to take.

Key #131

Our elders are the queens and kings of life, learn from their failures and success as if they are the only ones who can teach life.

Key #132

The frustration of this bubble can either progress you or decline you. Which way you want to go?

Key #133

Don't accept nothing of nobody, except for them to be themself.

Key #134

What is really, real?

Key #135

Not every situation is a situation. Stop looking for food in an empty pantry. If you can't see that you are the snake in the room when you think everybody is out to get you then your mind has no sanity.

Key #136

Privacy is like a nfl hail marry only 97% of the time will it be caught. We talk too much about nothing so we never die with a bit of the truth left only to one's self.

Key #137

Stop making decision from the eyes. See what can't be seen.

Key #138

The process is the builder of joy, stop crying over the build-up called work it makes the joy real.

Key #139

Stop being so comfortable with being comfortable.

Key #140

Everything you lust for, you don't have to lie in bed with.

Key #141

If the water is no good why drink from it? Why keep putting

poison in your body, when you know it's not good for you but you ignore the signs. The water was brown yesterday as it is today.

Key #142

Everybody has their on view of life, you can never change a narrow view of life so stop trying.

Key #143

Even when life brings a flood of craziness don't be a victim go build a boat and sail right on over it.

Key #144

I've become insensitive to problems to the point where I confront them as soon as it occurs not caring about the outcome but concerning myself with getting out of the problem quickly and not allowing it to linger on.

key #145

Turn the tv off and sit with god for five minutes.

Key #146

If you see it in the dark, it will never become life.

Key #147

If you continue to tell yourself you are of nothing, you will always see yourself as nothing. You will never grow into something greater.

Key #148

Set your goals so high, you have no choice but to fly.

Key #149

The self educated man can maneuver just as well or better than a university educated man. The goal is to study the wonders of the world and develop the second largest muscle in your body other than your heart, the brain.

Key #150

They will tell you anything that you want to hear, that never matters to a sound minded human being. The only thing that matters is the vision that god gave you.

Key #151

Be still and listen to the direction of god and mind.

Key #152

It's not about the money, it's about the experience.

Key #153

Think deeper than the cover, and you will find the answer.

Key #154

Quick decisions lead to quick failure.

Key #155

Business is for the consistent, not the impassioned.

Key #156

The goal is not the end goal but the first of many goals for the rest of your life.

Key #157

Own one hundred percent of everything you create not 90%.

Key #158

Be creative and innovative that is the only way to wealth.

Key #159

The intoxication of the brain does not just come from drugs and alcohol, it also comes from the environment that surrounds you and what you consume intellectually.

Key #160

All I wanted was clean water, but here I am digging in the dirt still trying to build a well after all this time. However it's been raining the last three days but still no water.

Key #161

To have the information and not live the information.

Key #162

Were you born for the Rolex, or the growth of love? Are you here to create or work? Or were you creatively designed to work?

Key #163

All the coaches were at the game but none of them brought their playbook.

Key #164

Never feel uncomfortable being you.

Key #165

We are at clean water again. Only peace! The day is anew. Be at service and extend your hands to others.

Key #166

Tell me what you are thinking when you talking to me. Tell me the truth don't soften the blow.

Key #167

You can't win a team sport if nobody passes the ball.

Key #168

Negativity shelters insecurities.

Key #169

Innovation is not to cause more death, it's to preserve more life.

Key #170

Is it the fear or exhaustion that makes us not want to get out of bed. It is extremely easy to confuse the two.

Key #171

Stop counting what's in your pockets and start looking at how many people you helped today for free. Extend your hands to others and you will never go hungry.

Key #172

If you can't lead your feet to the ground then you can't give anyone directions.

Key #173

When the day starts out negative, don't live in that negativity rise above it and keep smiling you will end up winning the day.

Key #174

Reject the process, love the sacrifice.

Key #175

Change the world, not the size of your pocket and everything will be provided for you.

Key #176

Don't believe what is not to be understood.

Key #177

Raise the kids in an academic environment that nurtures

innovation and freedom.

Key #178

Every morning look in the mirror and tell yourself, "I love you"!

Key #179

So when they say you don't matter leave the situation and watch them hurt from the void.

Key #180

To hear the excuses, of why certain goals can't be accomplished is no longer valid. I wrote this book on a fire 8 inch tablet. All one hundred and eighty keys. As long as there is determination, creativity and desire all things are possible, with god guiding you along the journey.

Author Info:

Email: Woodard Holdings@gmail.com

Facebook: Woodard Holdings

Other Books Authored: Available where books are sold

188 Keys

Words I never said to my son about money and credit

The blueprint to being limitless

The blueprint to power leadership

Buy, Hold, Sell Automated trading for every income

"All this would not be possible without my mother."